Seahorses

HAZEL FREW

Seahorses

Shearsman Books
Exeter

Published in the United Kingdom in 2008 by
Shearsman Books Ltd
58 Velwell Road
Exeter EX4 4LD

www.shearsman.com

ISBN 978-1-905700-61-5

Acknowledgements:
Some of the poems (or versions of) in this collection have been published or
accepted for publication by the following, to whose editors and publishers
I am most grateful: *Air, Clockwork Scorpion* (Rack Press 2007), *Cutting Teeth,
Fras, Orbis, Painted, spoken, Poetrypf, The Rialto, Nerve, New Writing Scotland,
Poetry Scotland, Pulsar* and *Riverrun.*

Special thanks to Richard Price, Alexander Hutchison and Nicholas Murray
for their support, advice and friendship.

Cover image, *Head-foot*, copyright © Delia Baillie, 2005.
www.deliabaillie.co.uk

CONTENTS

To Joy, Tom and Graham.

SEAHORSES

SEAHORSES

Hopes are
seahorses,
elegant urchin.

Bubbles in glasses
treble clefs.

There's a spring
of them bursting
Ka-pow-ing daily.

Despite the
furrows
in my face.

CLOCKWORK SCORPION

I dreamed I had
a clockwork scorpion
who scuttled slowly
about my limbs
in black shiny armour.

Japanned like
a sideboard,
rock hard
in my hands
but friendly
as a budgie
on my shoulder,
a remotely controlled
conversation piece.

Upturning
this black turtle
I switched
my new pet off
at the belly battery
like a walkie-talkie doll.

But the scorpion
who gained
in confidence and stealth
chattered and spun
quickly around the room
too fast to track
with the naked eye.

Rally driving
claw clicking
snap-jawed
a set of false teeth
incising
across carpet.

Then taking
to flight
it launched itself
at my neck
and knocked me
clean off my feet.

SPIKED ON A SPINDLE

Meeting on
the street
to listen to you
and watch your
large lip quiver
succulently
(from wetting
the skein my prince
from whetting
the thread)
spiked on a spindle
you pay the ferryman
and dream of a
moonlit crossing.

The Virago

They knitted corn dollies
and pentagrams
in their spare time
and cast spells
on visiting tradesmen

blowing them off roofs
or rolling gas
bottles at them
splintering fingers
in slammed doors

those two sisters
darning up fate
like odd socks
stretched across
knobbly fingers

making effigies in wax
and talking
with familiars,
malevolently

scheming termagants
sharing the eye
in liver spotted hands
and leaving
woven misery
on boilers.

HALE-BOPP

Projecting a dusty beam
At the earth's cinema;
A falling snowball
Waiting to be caught.

You open your bright eye
at us but never wink.

A hole in the sky
spraying an iridescence
of question about you.

Your two tails sail
on the tide of felicity
around the cosmic pancake
which is your heart.

A dropped scone
in the night sky.

BUCEPHALUS

Positively prehistoric.
Arched on all fours
in the rays of the moon.

Cancroid limbed.
Sprouting hair
then elongating,
Wolf-snouting.

Bison backed and
heavy shouldered
painted onto cave-walls
in the dance of flame.

Spear carrying nomad
Bedouin Boudicca.
Bucephalus
beneath thigh.

GARMENTS

I put myself on
dressing my bones
in a guise of you

It's not simply
that I put you on
like a garment
when threatened,
welcomed or disarmed

It's more the case
I am you to my core

Learned in my walk,
talk and expectations
warped in my fingernails,
snail-trails and apologies

I can see myself
proffering tea
like some nanny-goat

Fussing over plates
and napkins,
coasters under glasses

I catch sight of myself
but I see you.

EMERGING

Emergency emergence
somewhere undetected:
dormant, quiet, damp.

Pushes a hand
from the light
in the stomach.

Tests a finger
in the air.

I kept the baby
in my pocket
sheathed in paper
aluminium foil.

Willow branches
declare starts.

Each tiny day
the serrated lid
of a new country.

DOING TIME

The steady conveyance
of breakfast,
dinner and tea.

This is the format:
the schedule
to embark upon.

Discussing basil
black or green olives
garlic or chilli.

Fretting the necks
from leeks;
stalking tomatoes.

Hesitant phone-calls then
to mull over cheeses,
lukewarm macaroni,
the vices of pastry.

His fingers chop
fine elegant slithers
an igloo of onion
Ready to fry.

Corners please.
One stirring:
one tasting.

Each
hardly aware
of another.

COCKTAILS:

MARTINI

Nub olive
in an oily ellipse
Fully bitten
first sip.

MARGARITA

Crispy lip
Orange tempered
Hot device.

BLOODY MARY

Twisted anchovy
winding Worcester
Tabasco rapier
Hit of blood.

Woo Woo

Hands n' knees
woo-woo.

Fast-slow
woo-woo.

Nose-dive
woo-hoo.

An apricot
fall.

COLLECTOR

Something about
the cut
goblet, beaker
flute, flagon
that turns
an honest
girl into
a thief.

Rolling in
my palms
testing
weight
imagining
the taste
each shape
will assume.

Minerals made
complicit
slipping tumblers
into pockets
high-balls
down my legs
each token shot
illicit.

BABY LOVE

Some people who need love
get themselves a baby
But a baby can only receive love
it gives none back to the giver
whose arms lie empty
and aching in the night
As the baby sleeps
with its back to the wall.

INTERLUDE

You are
as light as web
flexible
and thin

Gossamer
tattooed
acne-dusted

Concave skin
chattering
in the heat
of a two day fad.

Asparagus

In the garden
with the chairs
upended
(presumably
in-avoidance of rain)
I watch you bend
into plastic
moulding yourself.

Keen to peel
off a t-shirt
eager to kick
off your jeans.

How unusual
to eat
asparagus-soup
in the scalding
daylight.

Pinioned
on a bench
admiring
mother's
handy-work.

Spiders sleepy
bees and wasps
larking.

What a curious
afternoon.

The hours
the speed
the train
the offering.

The out-of-the-blue
company.

August Moon

Onyx
Easter egg
new-born
in clouds.

Smudged
monochrome,
urging an
appearance
on the brow.

Under hills
yellow-lamps
strewn.

The garden
glittering-damp.

You taking me
on the bench.

PIROUETTE

In the hospital
in the final
counting of days

You saw ballerinas
waltzing
hand in hand

Their little
numbered bibs
pinned to skin

Ambulancing home
you settled down

Never quite making
it to the kitchen

To die suddenly
in your pyjamas

The indignity
of jelly

A set of teeth
rolling on the floor

Medical hands
exposing smooth,
ageless breasts.

RETICULUM

A sticky damp
A hole in my back
Just above the hip
a keyhole

A kidney boxed
in ribbons
Smooth reticulum
Shaped like a bean
with an insect sheen

This aubergine
Transplanted inside
Keep thumbs aside
No probing the wound
The stick of cloth to clots
All irritants

I pulled at your face
to make you see
Tugged at your lobes
couldn't make you listen

Dissipating into snow
The keening wind
Blowing ice
around your parcels.

CAVIAR

There's something
fishy about you
carp, perch, pike

You slither in
the murk
on the surface
friendly enough

A damp cell
clammy skin
Even on top
of sky-rise
you still reek
of basement

The earth at
the bottom
of ponds
suits you best

Spitting sprats
through clench

Submerged
before the emerging
fanfare

Almighty womb
slipping caviar.

PEEK A BOO!

Peek a boo!
I spy some flaws
The constellation
of moles
Adorning your
bloodhound lip.

If a bow-wow
can't be bought
Why not craft one
with sheer force
of will?

If you are naked
Who's to say
you aren't clothed
in finery?

The plaudits
will sail you
to ambitions quay.

The emperor
awaits
with open arms.

A crowd
admiring the metaphor,
the suit,
the rigged hand.

FISH WHISKERS

A golden fish flew out of its tank
and inch-wormed across the floor

In panic three women chased
after his great tail and fish whiskers

Two, bending and clapping
on their knees
as if calling to a pet dog

The fish had by now
curled his way into the hall

So the bravest of the three
grabbed a raincoat beige and plain
to wind it in, until swaddled
spooled inside rainwear

Later, she swore the fish talked
his low voice floundering

Something about air killing you
something like that.

CORRIDORS

Familiar corridors
white-gilled passages

Waiting in chairs
for nurses in green

Dropped back
mouth clamped
over-stretched

Open wide
for injections

Look away
from blood-letting,
agar, tubes, pipettes

Resigned anaesthesia

Clinical eyelashes
peep from beyond
paper-masks
ready to hypnotise
with drill, swabs, scythes

Polished cutlery
for the open gum.

SWEAT

The second day
brings sweats
to be dried
by a hairdryer
and a constant
reaching
for towels
Thereafter,
insomnia
can creep
around
for weeks
With cystitis,
weight loss
and a blessed
inability
to speak.

STICK

Stick me apart
my heart lies thick
on the stalk.

Its recesses hissing
and quick.

Wet pistons boiling
and I destroying
this thing I love.

These suggestions
fleet on tongue
nougat to the taste.

Have mercy ebbing
that never leads
to shelter.

Shirked or avoided
a span truncated.

A life measured
by age gap.

Soma

I have allowed you
close enough

Only this far
and stop

This is precision

What have I done?
where are all
the grains?

Gone, sieved
downward

Shard, shingle
into stain

This is our lot
this is not a lot
the tally is fail

We live
to give space

A line so fine
it's stretching
credibility

Be my nurse
tend my skin
my mind agonised.

For pity's sake
this thing on paper,
this half moon calf
on the ground
is spaghetti

This mess
is only appetite

Yet combining
each string would
summon the swing
of an acrobat.

SNAIL

Each day
tastes of a dream
once had

Once awake
The quaking
withdrawal, a sea, a gulf

The shell in my pocket
a memory
of a brief quell
in Portobello

The past between us
insurmountable.

WASP BLANKET

The heat when it hits
starts at the rib
radiant solar plexus
lava on neck.

Next come spitfires
shoals made of insect
a squadron of stingers
netting the dark.

Yellow-tail landing
wasps bang on target
face, body, hands
a blur.

Peel and examine
trap in a blanket
the serve of a light bulb
batted above.

The mind is a furnace
electrical synapse
fuse and confusion
blown right apart.

Thrum

A childish possession,
a play thing.

A yo-yo
on a string.

Kept in a pocket
and dangled down
when no other diversion
can be found.

The guitar
in your hands
detail transmission.

Maple and walnut
in preference to skin.

Thrum
with a vague look
to the cloudy distance.

Then, the occasional
yo-yo
stop-go, emotive.

Up and down
smile versus frown,
clown into cad.

Those ossified moods
mahogany.

Cold and red
to the touch.

Temper exploding
tetchily.

Knitted cross-brow
seethe, into hush.

BLISTER

Teal silk
to show you up.

Have you been
to Chinatown, you sigh?

An irrational inquiry
shot from the hip.

To think I was willing
to be a pod.

To ripen russet
before your eyes.

That it's come
to this.

Blister
not bliss.

A friction of silence
ruining the night.

Spike Versus Paw

The ladybird and the rabbit
both giants of their trade

line up, begin to race
beetling, hopping
scratching, loping
spike versus paw.

Driven by a toddler
egging each position

and me
trying to save
them from extinction

in the process
getting bitten,
better get your mitts on.

Time to stand clear
not interfere
in things spoken
when it's best to listen.

ARCHANGEL

An angel, arch
Culture-kit junky
Bosoms plump
Cheeks rosettes
Froideur chilly as
Baltic schuss.

OBSIDIAN

Smooth and round
cold warming

Veined black
masculine marble

TURQUOISE

A bite
of ocean

A nugget
of green

RHODONITE

pink pink pink
future magnet

karmic rake
layered sand

Drip Drying

He used to sniff clothes pegs
swim-wet with detergent
under the drip drying trees

Looking up only
as a thunder clap train
rocked the rock-garden

Running cold fingers
where she had
before him

Smoothing creases
sighing out loud

One large tear
ellipsing an eyelid

Brimming
swollen, salty
on an upward face

Fore fingers
catching zipper

The receiver
in his fly.

Bathing Mantis

Awkward limbs
pin-head joints

Knees doubled
in an effort
to squat
on a bony arse

Emersion is
short - the
gangrenous
rubber tube

The whole
place drips
like a candle

Here you
perch naked
— a cricket
blending

Spooling
yourself in a
tiny towel.

THE WORST

The worst part
of me

Emerging
like a demon

Avenging
itself on a fly

Legs flailing
on a severed torso

Screaming
vengeance into air

Making
hands into fists

Worrying
over has-beens

Emerging
nasty, nasty
nastier still

The brooding
only an accession.

Voodoo

I call voodoo
on you

Cause you
can't do this
to me

You can't
give this
and be
untainted

So voodoo
will have
to do

The very
sentence
for you

Proves
patience.

DAMAGED

We are all
damaged goods
she said.

Broken crockery
slate, flint, stone.

It's slippery
inside your head.

The realisation
dawns slow.

Black clouds
move as cattle
against the
turquoise horizon.

Russian Doll

The three of us
sat in talk of
Govan streets
in the thirties
when families
lived close
and old faces
lost stood alive

And I saw myself
filter through
each of you
we, the Russian dolls

Fitting snugly
together

One from inside
another
in startling
similarity

Grandmother,
mother
and daughter.

YELLOW ROSES

She might live in a fairy tale cottage
with yellow roses all around the door.

Chinese lanterns swing on clotheslines
and we sit on stripy deckchairs
with you showing off your hairs
in a melting pot of observations,
hesitations; wild animations.

The trees flutter and the grass is damp.
I study the tenement from
the basement up and worry
about how thin you are.

How tired you are on
removed, currentless days.
Yet more alive with bright starlight
in a world of my own design.

BLUE PEARS

Pears
like cocks

Draped
across dish

Languid
on thigh

Smooth
circumcised flesh.

FACE FITTING

I'm wearing your
face again

Your features
fit over mine
like linked fingers
(can anybody see it?)

I'm looking
with your eye
and talking
with your tongue
(surely they must see it)

My mouth feels
like your mouth
I want to laugh

I'm sculpted
around you

You're arched
in my heels
coiling in my heart

A growling promise
in my open arms.

SHIRT LIFTING

I don't want to
let go of you
sometimes
in the street
I want to kiss
your neck
and stare
and run my hands
up, under your
shirt onto your
smooth back
in the open air.

Portrait

You sleep
with a smirk
on the side
of your face

Nose and eye
Salvador Dali

An eyebrow
etches to temple

The ear to follow
sugar candy

Hair tousled
as if previously
arranged by tweezers

Neck, shoulders
a white slope

With brittle black
hairs as trees.

SLEEP

The night is
inky-dark-black
The wind waves
its arms about
The room is in
the usual place
the usual time
Duvet and cover
The comforting
wooden frame
I've always
believed in bed

LOLLIPOPS

On a walk within
the springing park
crocuses push up
against the blades
like purple lollipops
and he smells like
a digestive biscuit
on my arm.

The sky is musty
grey as cold ashes
Damp trees
slope off towards
the curdling river
yellow and thick
as milky tea
Like a cup for me
to dunk you into.

KITE

There's a dozing moth
folded in the slats
of a tipsy venetian.

The heat is retreating
light inches backwards
edging away from us.

Underneath lies the kite
you spread out,
rolling the plastic tail
that I hoped to find
breath for in the sky.

I see its angles
pointing at me
through an open door.

There isn't time now
with all the shock and leaving
and things better unsaid.

CATCH

I've stopped talking
a ventriloquist throws
my words at you
from somewhere over there   >>

At first I thought
you were joking
playing along.

True you couldn't see
glass in my eyes
Couldn't tell flesh
from bone.

Hollowed inside
let a voice
sound outside.
But am I there or here?

Worst of all
to realise
you didn't see
me leave.

WHITE

A sharing
has been
severed

The home
is gone

The hearth
empty and cold

That place
by the sea
windy, desolate

Concrete cottages
slabs
stones

Your gate
swinging open
in the dim
autumn light

A white limousine
drawing slowly
away

Maybe

Move
fast enough

Maybe
I can see
you in the
corner
of my eye

Hear your
laugh
on the street

Run after you
in time

Not always
the periphery

A snowflake
melting

SPACES

letting go
by living

learning to
breathe

tricks of
the trade
in those
spaces
without you

a clamp
firmly
about
my ribs.

EXCHANGES

I dialled
your number
by mistake
today

It's these
little repetitions
that stab
at my heart.

THE THREE STOOGES

The first
rib-snapper.

The second
crib-jammed narcissus.

The third
wood-lost.

She, kitchen-maid
teacher, friend, preacher.

Back-bending
jaw breaking.

Serving in servitude
to the whimsy
and the mood.

How come she
never saw
it coming?

The first
elbow-raging.

The second
pussy-eating.

The third
self-doubting.

Believable and sweet
promising protection.

So much promise
gone with knowledge.

With the morning
comes rejection.

Chickens

When I was little
you took us
adventuring
in a gold
Hillman Hunter

You told
many things
drove us afar

Easter-egg
chocolate
melting on
the back shelf

Spilling on
rustic-dyke lanes
and by-ways
our car-boat afloat

Car shadow sundial
suns length or lack

Moon tales,
remote hospitals
where patients
count their steps
like chickens
on a car lot.

Cook the Cat

Your applause please
gentlemen
for the young
vivisectionist
Who with an
intensity
of Cartesian
detachment
Successfully
cooked
the cat alive
beneath
the angle-poise
Proving
once again
that sugar
changes under
conditions of heat.

THE CHICKEN FACTORY

It's a sick wind
rendering
sinew, beak, feathers
into air

Leftover melt-down
fed back
to chicks

Wind a scarf
around my face
keep out the scent

In the killing
the long knives
slice

The unlucky ones
boiled alive

Grown on
a postage stamp
to be shocked
into light

Upside down
Boxed, broken

Loaded lorries
ferry the new
to a bloody
destination.

FLY TIME

The dance of the flies
has finally begun
The aphids
have been called
They're warming up
as we speak.

Liberated; regarding
us from toilet walls
Wise to pesticide and
indifferent to missiles.

They spin on my
window sill
each morning.

And it doesn't matter
how many you
can kill, Jack
slaying is pointless.

There are always more
black-bodies buzzing
humming, head-butting glass.

Wheeling; knotting
each other up like
magical magnets.

Is this courtship?

These are the dances
and romances in the
summer of the flies.

HUNGRY SWANS

From choppy waters
come translucent feet
graceful over pebbles
Membranes flattening
onto sea debris like
smooth wet netting.

Winding their long necks
toward us
Slowly and surely
approaching
Emerging upright
Pedestrians of the sea
Plump marionettes
held by invisible thread.

We feed bread
to these dappled swans
Throwing crumbs
up into the air
for the acrobatic gulls
who catch effortlessly.

Across the bay
a lighthouse blinks
Winking at the cold day
A lifeboat bobs
in the water.

All is tranquillity
as the river stretches
her legs out to sea.

SEALS

This beach
was made
for us to
skim across

This bay
is a place
and time
for you and me

Swept and carried
on the drifting sand

Together here
hands warm
smiling eyes
gazing into
the water
for seals.